For my mother, Eileen Heasley, who prayed.

to me
...with Arms wide opened
"Love me", He says.
CONSISTENCY
GRACE LOVE, JOY
COMPLETE
THY WILL
HOLY SPIRIT
24-7
PRAYER
HOLY FIRE COME
BRING MORE LIFE
INTO THE MOVEMENT
THANK YOU
KEEP ON BREATHING!
DO NOT FEAR

BE my LOVE!
my FRIEN
TRUTH · HOPE
STRENGTH · J
PEACE · CONFI
I HAVE ALL
IN YOU .
GRACIA
THANK Y
THANK
THANK Y
· L O V E ·

HOLD ME LORD

·HiS BLOOD PAYED MY RANSOM·

TABLE OF CONTENTS

ACKNOWLEDGMENTS

Thank you to Carla, Robert and Andrea for all your hard work and input. Tracy, Ellis and Dan, you are all so wonderful.

These people were instrumental in making this project happen: Rebecca Hunt, for hunting down prayers; Valerie Rush, for typing so many of them up; Dan King, for the great book from Canada; Lisa and Byron Borden, for their artwork and encouragement; Emma Woods, for inspiring me to do this; everyone at Diss Christian Community Church; Shelli Haight from Buckner Ragsdale; everyone at Revelation Church Chichester; Anne at River of Mercy, the West London Boiler Room; and the guys at Reading, especially Andy Freeman.

Pete, Samie, Daniel and Hudson, thank you for your time, hospitality, input and inspiration at key stages.

Ibiza people—you made the dream a reality: Steve and Dawn Jeffery, Fiona Roberts, Indya Hanlon, Johanna Pahl and everyone else who joined us on 24-7 missions teams in 2006. These stories are our stories.

There are so many others I could thank. As a movement, from 2000 to 2006 we have seen 3,731 prayer rooms registered in 63 different nations (many more have not registered), with 626,808 hour-long slots of prayer filled. That equates to over three and a half billion minutes spent in prayer worldwide! Thank you to everyone who took a risk and ran a prayer room. We would be nowhere without you.

This book is just the beginning of an ever-growing generational heart-cry. These prayers are snapshots and by no means the whole picture. To the nameless people from all over the world who have contributed to this project, this is your book, and we thank you. Your prayers will bring others closer to the Maker, who we know listens.

God's Graffiti

Pete Greig

The party was pumping. Everyone was having a good time. A *very* good time, if you know what I mean. Suddenly there was a scream—everyone froze, staring in disbelief at the wall. Terrified, they watched as a disembodied hand appeared right before their eyes.

God, it seemed, had decided to do some graffiti, right there on the plaster by the lamp stand. And this is what God had decided to write: *Mene. Tekel. Peres.*

Breathless, they located the old-man prophet and summoned him to the scene. He stumbled in, bleary with sleep, and somehow made sense of the writing on the wall. If the hand was to be trusted (and it seemed impolite to doubt it), the days of the king were numbered by divine decree. Apparently, the "host with the most" would soon be toast. And sure enough, "that very night Belshazaar, king of the Babylonians, was slain" (Daniel 5:30).

* * *

God did graffiti. Jesus drew in the sand. Cavemen painted the walls of their caves, and Michelangelo had a pretty good go at the ceiling of the Sistine Chapel.

When Brian Heasley first contacted me to tell me that he had been moved to tears by a prayer written on the walls of his church, he suggested the name *Writing on the Wall* as a title for a compilation of such prayers from around the world. The 24-7 Movement has dozens of prayer rooms on the go all the time in all sorts of weird locations all over the world, and it occurred to Brian as he wept that night that there must be other prayers like the one he had just read. Prayers that impact people. Words that help us be honest with God. Would it be possible to get some of these together, he wondered?

A few days later I jumped on a plane from England to America, where I was due to speak to some churches and hang out with some friends. To my surprise, my old friends Robert and Andrea Jobe in Tulsa, Oklahoma—knowing nothing of Brian's suggestion—approached me with exactly the same idea. They even had the same title in mind. Three different people on two different continents in just one week had come up with an identical concept: a book of non-religious prayers by ordinary people, full of passion and embarrassing honesty. This random collection of psalms and lamentations reflecting the spirituality of the emerging culture could, they said, be called *Writing on the Wall*—an echo of the day God Himself showed up at a party and did graffiti.

Understanding the Spiritual Significance of a Cereal Packet

I've never found prayer particularly easy. It's ironic, because I help lead an international prayer movement, but it's true nonetheless. I'm bad at prayer.

As a result of this spiritual incompetence, I always appreciate books full of ready-made prayers that help me in my devotional life and trigger my imagination with new language for our shared human experiences. As a teenager, I often turned to a hopelessly uncool book of poems called *Prayers of Life* by a Catholic priest named Michelle Quoist. These days, my bedside table carries a book of Celtic daily prayers and another compilation of Franciscan meditations. By my toilet you will find a book of prayers from Brennan Manning and *The Diary of an Old Soul* by George MacDonald. Last week I sat in a recording studio in my friend's basement, thumbing through a dusty old copy of *The Book of Common Prayer*.

However, my favorite prayer book of all time is the Psalter, King David's outrageously honest compilation of worship, intercession, grumbling and gratitude. There are very few churches today that would allow anyone to be as publicly angry and distressingly uncertain as David repeatedly is in the psalms. On the other hand, those more thoughtful groups that do permit a little messy questioning and occasional moaning often seem embarrassed by David's terminal "charismania"—his irrepressible eruptions of jubilation, his moments of religious imperialism, his naked dancing in the street.

From AIDS to a Slice of Pizza

I like prayer books, but the one in your hands is different from the norm. Most contemplative titles are written by educated mystics in rarefied environments, light-years away from the rush and bustle of normal society. Such books are exquisite precisely because they are compiled by deep people, clever people: clerics and hermits, poets and zealots.

But this book represents the meditations of a messy spirituality, the prayerful ramblings of ordinary people who never intended their thoughts to be widely read. These are the prayers of the meek, the poor in spirit, those who hunger and thirst for righteousness. Some might not even call themselves Christians, but they believe in prayer and have dared to post their heart-cries on the Internet, on university and church walls and even, in one situation, on the wall of a brewery.

The eighteenth-century poet Samuel Taylor Coleridge concludes his classic Gothic masterpiece, *The Rime of the Ancient Mariner*, with a simple observation:

> *He prayeth best who loveth best*
> *All things, both great and small.*

The prayers in this book really are about "all things, both great and small." There's a prayer about AIDS and another one about a slice of pizza. A kid thanks God for rainbows while a teenager cries out for help with her compulsion to self-abuse. An ex-con meditates on the meaning of freedom while a Portuguese philosopher contemplates the deep spiritual significance of a cereal packet. These are prayers of life, *all* of life—the shadows as well as the light. Brian Heasley appropriately describes it as "naked prayer."

Soft Whispers to the Ear

People in every culture around the world and in every generation down the ages have always prayed. Archaeologists have found evidence of the human compulsion to worship and pray in artifacts dating back to the dawn of time. Anthropologists testify to the universal centrality of prayer in both the most primitive societies and the most sophisticated cultures of the world.

And even in that tiny, self-obsessed segment of human history known as "modern" and "Western," where the ridiculous notion of atheism has been proposed and espoused by a few, the God-impulse prevails. In our brave new world, something primal moves us to build shrines by the roadside, to cover tragedies with candles and handwritten cards, to download music encoded with heart-cries to God, to upload our prayers into celestial cyberspace.

Gloucester Cathedral, which broods over the rolling hills of the English Cotswolds, has been a place of prayer for 1,300 years. In the cathedral's Whispering Gallery, you can find writing on a wall where one intercessor, long ago, was moved to make an inscription in the ancient stones:

> *Doubt not but God who sits on high,*
> *Thy secret prayers can hear;*
> *When a dead wall thus cunningly*
> *Conveys soft whispers to the ear.*

Dead walls can indeed "convey soft whispers to the ear" as secret prayers ascend. Jesus says that God hears the mumbling of tax collectors and ignores the posturing of Pharisees. He is moved by the humility of the meek and weak, whose prayers, we may be sure, rise to God on high.

You've bought this book (let's face it, it would be a weird one to steal), but you have not yet made it your own. These prayers will slowly become yours over the coming weeks and years as your reflection makes simple words profound and public prayers secret again. And as you reflect, perhaps—like that pilgrim in Gloucester Cathedral—you will be allowed that rare surprise: the unmistakable sound of a still, small voice from somewhere and nowhere that whispers with you an impassioned *Amen*.

> *Now to him who is able to do immeasurably more than*
> *all we ask or imagine, according to his power that is at*
> *work within us, to him be glory in the church and in*
> *Christ Jesus throughout all generations, for ever and ever!*
> *Amen.*
> EPHESIANS 3:20-21

Naked Prayer

Walls always seem to get written on—ever been to a public toilet that had nothing to say?

I suppose I've always been surrounded by writing on walls. From ornate murals to clumsy graffiti in the school yard, the pain, passion and—yes—prayers of ordinary people have always intrigued me. Growing up in Northern Ireland, the elaborate paramilitary graffiti of East Belfast formed the backdrop for much of my childhood. As a young man in and out of prison, I read the thoughts (both primal and profound) of fellow inmates, anonymously etched on the paintwork of cells. As a homeless person, I occasionally slept in bus shelters and marveled at people's need to express their anger and creativity (or just advertise for some customers). As a father of two, the walls of my home have been frequently adorned with crayon, felt-tip marker and jam. And now as a pastor (it's been a long journey from Belfast!), I sit in prayer rooms surrounded by people's private longings, written out on the walls for all to see.

As I sat in the 24-7 prayer room in Norfolk, England, not too long ago, I was moved to tears. The raw prayers of young pilgrims scrawled on the walls touched me—they were painful, passionate, angry and grateful, but most of all they were honest. (And believe me, if growing up in Northern Ireland taught me anything, it was that we could all do with a lot more honesty and a little less religion.)

Sitting there, I started to think, *What if these modern-day psalms could be collected?* Surely it would be inspiring to see these written thoughts put together in a style more *street* than *chapel*. Maybe such words, written in an honest, non-religious style, could move thousands deeper in their own dialogues with God.

Rude Graffiti

Graffiti: A rude decoration inscribed
on rocks or walls[1]

Rude: Rough in manners or behavior; unmannerly;
of a primitive simplicity[2]

The resulting book is not a work of literary genius. It's not a collection of the musings of intellectuals. It's rude graffiti—prayer in honest, naked form.

There is nothing contrived about this compilation of prayers, written in private moments far from prying eyes. Two thousand years ago, some ordinary men asked Jesus to teach them to pray. His advice? "Find a quiet, secluded place so you won't be tempted to role-play before God. Just be there as simply and honestly as you can manage" (Matthew 6:6, *THE MESSAGE*). For Jesus, prayer was about honesty, simplicity and privacy.

The prayers here are glimpses of the insatiable longings of a few hearts—a hundred or so prayers that are whispers of the heart-cry of a generation. There are poems, simple phrases, desperate cries, songs and love letters. A few are so disturbingly candid that you may feel uncomfortable reading them.

24-7 prayer rooms are places for spiritually naked prayer, which is probably why they are springing up all over the world. Much of what goes on there is not written down. For some who come to pray, their hour is a good, long cry. For others, it is an hour of silence, of connecting with God. For others, a challenge—a stirring call to action. We have included some of the stories behind the prayers to inspire and provoke you. Some artwork has also been included to give you a taste of the creative expression of prayers prayed through painting and drawing.

Jesus reminds us, "The world is full of so-called prayer warriors who are prayer-ignorant. They're full of formulas and programs and advice, peddling techniques for getting what you want from God. Don't fall for that nonsense. This is your Father you are dealing with" (Matthew 6:7, *THE MESSAGE*). This book bares the humble heart-cries of the tax collector, not the proficient prayers of the Pharisee. Names have been omitted because no one wrote these prayers to see them published. By featuring them in this book, we hope that these anonymous prayers can lead others in similar moments of worship, lament and intercession.

Graffiti Down the Ages

"The words of the prophets," observed Paul Simon, "are written on the subway walls." Graffiti is nothing new. Writing has been found on the walls of ancient sepulchers, catacombs and ruins. The eruption of Mount Vesuvius in A.D. 79 preserved graffiti carved into the walls of the Roman city of Pompeii, giving us a snapshot into the lives and times of the people who lived there—you can find insults, declarations of love and political statements.

Vikings graffitied walls in Rome, Varangians carved their runes in the Hagia Sophia, and ancient Irish Celtic communities had their own inscription language for writing in stone, called *Ogham*. The most renowned walls of the world have inscriptions etched into their stones: a section of the Great Wall of China was studied by archaeologists who found symbols representing love and peace written by soldiers, and the western side of the Berlin Wall was a virtual graffiti-scape, nearly every inch covered with carved and spray-painted messages.

Walls are written on to mark territory, to remember people and events, to broadcast messages of hope or revolution. In prisons and chapels, those who have gone before whisper their faded dreams, forsaken hopes and fervent desires through scribbles and scratches. Parents mark kitchen walls with the increasing heights of their children, holding memories of passing years and changing seasons of life.

Heart Graffiti of a Generation

Just as the graffiti of antiquity reveals the thoughts, feelings and aspirations of past generations, so too the prayers collected in this book hint at the underlying spirituality of generations coming of age today, generations that are sometimes written off as morally degenerate and spiritually illiterate by conservative branches of the Church. Abraham Lincoln once said, "I have been driven many times to my knees by the overwhelming conviction that I had nowhere else to go." Perhaps that is why these generations pray: Besieged by consumerism and undermined by modernity, they have ended up with "nowhere else to go," and they are turning to prayer.

Pope Pious XII said, "A person without prayer is like a tree without roots," and this book of prayers is a window into the roots of deep spiritual longing of the emerging culture. The angst of these generations is well documented, but very little has been said about the deep optimism of their spirituality. These are prayers from several continents and many cultures, yet there is a single heart-cry.

I remember lying in a prison cell, frightened and troubled and alone. I prayed—and even though I wouldn't have said that I was a Christian, I felt a strange presence invade the room and a sense of peace like I've never experienced since. I slept that night like a baby in his mother's arms. It was prayer and the presence of God, rather than the pulpit and preaching, that reached into my prison cell all those years ago. People who don't want to be preached at—and who aren't even sure if they believe in God—still believe in prayer.

The Beatitudes

We have categorized the prayers into chapters relating to the Beatitudes (see Matthew 5:1-12) because the words we have found on so many walls are the prayers of the poor in spirit, the mourning, the meek, the humble, the hungry and thirsty, the merciful, the pure in heart, the peacemakers, and even the persecuted. Our prayer is that these meditations, psalms and laments will move you the way they moved us and—more importantly—the way they moved the heart of God.

As you come to Him in "naked prayer" by reading the writing from walls around the world, may there be new prayers written secretly on the walls of your heart. God has promised to answer us in our distress, to enjoy the exuberance of our praise and to bless hopeless, hungry people like us with His presence forever. He reads the writing on the walls. We pray that wherever you are on your journey, you will speak to Him. He is listening.

Brian Heasley
Diss, England

Notes
1. Dictionary.com, s.v. "graffiti." WordNet® 2.1. Princeton University. http://dictionary.reference.com/browse/graffiti (accessed January 9, 2007).
2. Dictionary.com, s.v. "rude." Dictionary.com Unabridged (v 1.1), Random House, Inc. http://dictionary.reference.com/browse/rude (accessed January 9, 2007).

...HIS BLOOD PAYED MY RANSOM.

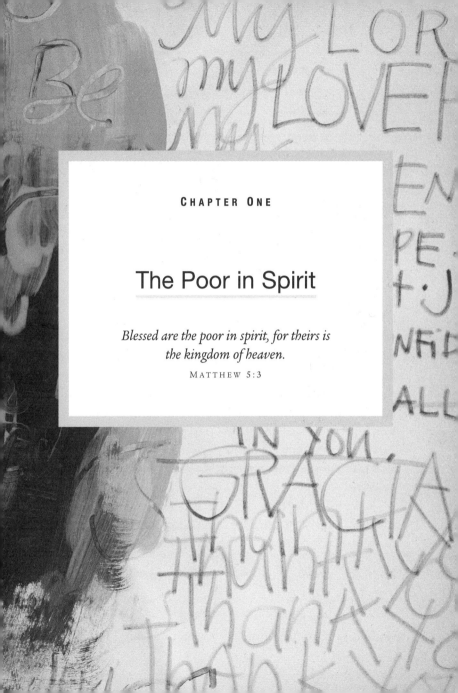

The Poor in Spirit

*Blessed are the poor in spirit, for theirs is
the kingdom of heaven.*

MATTHEW 5:3

I work for 24-7 Prayer on the European party island of Ibiza. My wife, Tracy, and I are part of a small team with a mission to show the love of God to residents, summer workers and holidaymakers. We have a particular emphasis on the West End of San Antonio, the second-largest municipality in Ibiza. The town is situated on a beautiful bay, renowned worldwide for its spectacular sunsets—and it has more clubs, pubs and bars per square mile than anywhere else in the whole of Europe!

During the holiday season, we become semi-nocturnal, spending the hours between 11 P.M. through to 5 A.M. walking the streets of San Antonio, praying with people to bring them a step closer on their journey to knowing God. Conversation with partygoers becomes less coherent by 3 A.M., but that's when the team can show God's love in a hands-on way by helping home (or to a hospital) those who are unable to help themselves due to overindulgence in alcohol or drugs. We also pray and worship God in some of the largest clubs in the world, carrying the light of God into places that desperately need it. Every summer, we are joined in our work by 24-7 mission teams who come to serve in the West End for two weeks at a time.

On top of all that, we run a 24-7 prayer room in San Antonio. Currently, there are over 1,200 prayers scrawled on cards that have been stuck to the walls, written by people we meet as we work. Most are written by people who wouldn't call themselves Christians. They are naked prayers, raw and disarmingly honest. The English poet Alfred Lord Tennyson wrote that "more things are wrought by prayer than this world dreams of," and in the depths of our beings, we know this to be true. When people fall on their face before God, broken and ready to admit their poverty of spirit, the Kingdom comes down to meet them.

The stories at the beginnings of the chapters of this book are not all my stories but a recollection of conversations and prayers from different individuals who have played a part in the summer work in the West End.

So Alone

These five prayers were written by a young woman
who had attempted suicide several times
after losing her sister.

I have many questions. Lots are difficult.
God, if my sister hadn't died, perhaps I wouldn't be where I am now.
Perhaps things would be better with my parents.
Maybe I would feel "normal"?
I might be able to talk (share my deep feelings with someone)
and not get so desperate. Maybe I wouldn't feel so empty.
So distant (afraid of what others may think of me).
I put on such a brave face yet inside I feel weak
and ready to crumble.
I can't get close to people, God. I take a long time to trust them.
And when I do, I am scared I will be rejected and pushed away.
I have such a fear when I look at old people.
It may sound strange, but—as I see their bodies and how
they have deteriorated—I feel scared.
I don't want to be like that.

* * *

I have tears trapped inside me from years and years.
I have bottled up feelings tangled inside.
I find it so hard to believe that anyone would love me—
You know, love me without any strings attached.
If I do something wrong—make any mistakes—
surely I should be punished? Made to feel small?

* * *

I was once in my mother's womb—
I felt the big closeness. Yet now I feel distant.
I don't feel close to anyone.
I haven't for years.
I've coped alone.
But now, God, I can't. I'm fed up. I give up.
I am so sick of being alone. I need peace.
My heart feels physically tangled up.
Twisted and torn, hurt and broken.

* * *

I ask you today to begin to heal me.
Save me before it's too late.
Out of anyone, you can.

* * *

I love you. Have your way in me.

(UNITED KINGDOM)
[REQUEST]

Wilderness

Even my prayers here seem not to go through.
The darkness is oppressive.
God, hear my cry.
I am so weary and miss that awareness of your presence.
Please lead me from the wilderness.
I want to follow.

(WAILING WALL, WWW.24-7PRAYER.COM)

[LAMENT, REQUEST]

Self-Harm

I just don't know what to do.
I don't know how much longer I can last.
I'm worried about next week with the eating and the cutting.
I just don't think I'll be able to make it.
HELP ME, GOD!
Isaiah 53:5 . . . by His wounds we are healed.

(CANADA)

[REQUEST]

Outside Looking In

Feeling so alone
In a crowded room
Hands are raised
"Worthy is the Lord to be praised"
And "blessed be your name"
Resound from the lips of others
Who are unaware of my pain
And are telling me what to believe
Without answering my questions.
They pray using "just" and
Multitudes of clichés
Obsessed, it seems, with sounding
Good and holy.
But they leave me like an outsider looking in
They call it the "good news"
Without putting themselves in others' shoes.

(UNITED KINGDOM)
[LAMENT]

Burnt Out

Help me not to feel so burnt out.
I don't feel like reading the Bible or praying, but I need you.

(UNITED STATES)
[REQUEST]

Feel Like a Fool

I'm not on top of anything right now.
I feel like a fool, a mess-up, like I belong nowhere.
It's cold in my heart, and I'm tired of this day-to-day life—
it just repeats itself every day.
Tired of my complacency and apathy.
Reinvent in my life what it means to be in love with you.
I realize how satisfying you are, and how nothing will
ever satisfy me like you. Everything is so
unknown right now, but you are known,
and I want to know you more.

(CANADA)
[LAMENT]

Tired

Oh God, please give me the strength to go on.

(UNITED STATES)
[REQUEST]

Mother's Rest

Lord, I pray for my friend.
Help her two little children to sleep through the night
so that she can get a good night's rest.
Give her the patience she needs with them,
and the wisdom to be a good mother.

(UNITED STATES)
[INTERCESSION]

.

Employment

I need a job. Please take the pressure of not knowing.
I cast this burden upon you once and for all
because I do not have the strength to carry this any longer.

(DENMARK)
[REQUEST]

Bad Day

Father, I'm having a bad sort of day today
and I need you with me.

(SPAIN)
[REQUEST]

Screwed Up

God, I know I have screwed up a lot.
I don't know why but you give me chance after chance.
At one time I said I wanted to be out of your family.
I said I didn't want to be a Christian anymore.
I turned down your love and your forgiveness.
Everything I was told was right, I tried to do the opposite.
I became hateful. I hated my life and my family.
It's so overwhelming.
You have opened my eyes again, Lord.

(CANADA)
[REPENTANCE]

Allergy

Father, I know it's a small thing but please could you heal
me from my hay fever. It's really dragging me down
and not responding much to medication at the moment.
Please heal me from it. Thank you.

(UNITED STATES)
[REQUEST]

Strength to Quit Drugs

Dear Lord, please give me and any other who
desires to live free of drugs
strength to stay clean and sober today.
I can't do it alone, so please God grant me the
freedom that I need.
In Jesus' name I pray, Amen.

(GERMANY)
[REQUEST]

Fear

I don't know what I'm afraid of sometimes, God.

(UNITED KINGDOM)
[REPENTANCE]

CONSISTE

RENEWAL

FEAR OF THE LO

PURITY persistance

protection GRACE LO

COMPLETE

THY WILL TROUGH

U.S. we ask.

THE HONOUR & GLORY IS ALL YOURS.

24

PR

HOLY SPIRIT;
WELCOME! WEL
WELCOME! COM

OH YOU WINDS
OF THE NORTH;
SOUTH, EAST;
WEST! COME
BREATHE MORE
LIFE INTO THE
BONES
GET THE
ARMY
GOING! S

...Let us k... [within heart shape]

JOY.

sharpen our EARS to hear your heartbeat, LORD!
We are here to listen,
sharpen our sight to see what you're up to!
We are here to COPY YOU
COME!

7
YER

SPIRIT SPIRIT SPIRIT Help your people.

THANK YOU FOR SHOWING UP! THANK YOU FOR ENCOURAGEING YOUR PEOPLE THANKYOU FOR GUIDE IN

WE WELCOME LIFE!

THANK YOU for a SP...

DON'T ABANDON YOUR... THE LORD SW...

HAND W...

HOLY FIRE COME!
BRING MORE LIFE!
INTO THE MOVEMENT!

k you FOR what has been, is, and are to...

FATHER DO NOT ABANDON
THIRST FOR HOLYNESS.
WELCOME. THIRST FOR HA THAN
WELCOME PRAYER & INTIMACY
WEL COME!

PASS
WO...

HOPE COME IN SP...

BONES

Those Who Mourn

Blessed are those who mourn,
for they will be comforted.

MATTHEW 5:4

I don't know how many times I hear this, but it is a lot: "Can you pray for my granddad, grandma, father, mother, brother, sister, friend or so and so who is dead?" What strikes me is the sheer force of the pain in this place. So many conversations start with apparent disinterest, and yet as we scratch just below the surface, out come the stories of hurt, abuse, searching and longing after something beyond.

Take Hans, a lovely German man we met one night. He was far from God, and yet something in him was urging him back toward the Father he didn't yet know. We talked for a while and heard about his dissatisfaction with life as he knew it now, his broken dreams of being a professional soccer player, his desire to connect with God. He let us pray for the pain in his knee, the pain in his stomach and the deeper emotional pain in his heart.

Or take another young man we met—or maybe it is more appropriate to say who we were ambushed by—one evening. As we walked down the street, he came running toward us, shouting, "Save me! Save me!" He was probably still off his face on something, and yet what he was shouting was truer than he knew. He talked briefly about the drugs he'd taken, but then was fascinated to hear that we believed in a God who *talks* to us, a God who brings comfort. Pain again there. Just below the surface, masked a little by the drugs, yet stirred up in him.

The depth of the sadness and emptiness that we see glimpses of here is mind-blowing. And yet, so is the goodness, faithfulness, persistence and mercy of the God whom these precious people don't yet know. We sense the heart of God daily as He searches and calls and woos His longed-for children back home to be comforted.

Boyfriend

Dear Lord! I need Your guiding in my trouble . . .
the more I try to reach him,
the more he refuses to listen.
I can't make him love You! Please help me!
How wonderful it would be to go to the church
together with him
but he won't even give it a shot.
He closed his heart to YOU, Lord,
and I can't open it without YOUR amazing love.
Guide me.

(THE NETHERLANDS)
[INTERCESSION]

Rhythm of Life

Lord Jesus, please set my heart at peace again.
My emotions are confusing me.
Give me back a normal appetite and sleeping pattern.
I want to love you more and not be so easily swayed.

(WAILING WALL, WWW.24-7PRAYER.COM)
[REQUEST]

Failed Again

Repentance
seems an empty word
when I face the truth
I've fallen.
Maybe I can fix this tomorrow
with sweet promises of devotion
Paint on a holy face
and look the part.
But this is a vicious circle
I'm caught in this compulsion
Behind my camouflage.
I'm calling for a Savior.
Can there be hope again,
when I've let you down once more?
Dare I believe you love me still,
and you'll forgive me one more time?

(SWITZERLAND)
[REPENTANCE]

Lost

Lord, I don't really know what to say.
You know me inside out.
I'm lost. Completely lost. I'm just floating about
doing my bit as I think I should
and not really knowing what I should be doing.

(UNITED KINGDOM)
[REQUEST]

Suicidal

I am feeling very depressed about my future,
I don't see it getting better and am contemplating
ending it, God help me.
Psalm 143:7: "Come quickly, Lord, and answer me,
for my depression deepens.
Don't turn away from me or I will die" (NLT).

(WAILING WALL, WWW.24-7PRAYER.COM)
[REQUEST]

Prayer of the Assaulted

I remember the lights, the sea, the sky
Thinking that You were busy for how long?
My entire godforsaken wretched twisted life
Alabaster saints and incense couldn't
keep me from memories
Of his strong hands, the crack of my jaw,
the falling in the grass,
The scent of smoke and fear on my skin.
I only ever asked You for death before.
Agonies of love forced, came quick
I was just a little girl really
And I had so many dreams
How was I to know that death was real?
He woke me in the middle of the night
Stroking my face and telling me lies
"Some people don't get to be happy
Us two, we're some of these.
Come here and give me a kiss

You know better than to refuse me."
Not an inch untouched, protesting unheard
The threat of the streets, alone in a word.
I was angry at You, renounced You in
white disinfected rooms
You could keep Your prayers and I would keep my doom
Sometimes you have to protect yourself, see
Sometimes you're all you've got
And when you're wretched and addicted, raped and beaten
Yourself doesn't count for a lot.
But there was a vein running through the desert
A rush of blood I could never deserve
I washed my feet with holy water
And walked away, one of Yours, Your daughter.

(WAILING WALL, WWW.24-7PRAYER.COM)
[LAMENT, THANKS]

Lost in Love

I lost my fiancée. Somehow we just broke
and I am shattered, hurt, angry, despairing and unsure
of how to get what I want.
I miss my love, the dreams we lost and the life
we were planning.
I don't know where you are taking our hearts.
Please rescue and restore our dreams.

(UNITED STATES)
[LAMENT]

Strip Me Bare

God, strip me bare
Remove my pride, fear, inhibitions,
false motives, lust, impatience,
complacency, greed and envy.
I am nothing on my own.
Strip me of everything that remains of my earthly nature
and reveal the sin in my life.
I don't want to live a complacent Christian life.

(CANADA)
[REPENTANCE]

Your X-Ray Affection

In silence and seclusion I sit and ponder God.
Tired and broken I consider my own worth and find none.
Every good deed in my life was secretly evil.
My heart is prideful and bitter.
I see this sin in my own life and with my own eyes
and think of how much worse it must look from
the perfect eyes of my savior.
Your love is amazing, Jesus!
How you can look on me with love
when I can't even keep the simplest of your
commandments astounds me.
In your sight I am laid bare. And yet there is still love.
You still love me.
Thank you. Thank you. I'm yours.
Thank you.

(CANADA)
[MEDITATION]

Someone Who Hears

There are times when all that makes sense
Is the pain I feel day by day.
Sometimes all that I desire is the end
The end of my life and emotions.
Sometimes I just want to curl up
Nice and tight into a little ball
Sometimes I can't believe
that there is anything good left.
I can't believe there is anyone
Anywhere
That is good.
It seems like everyone cares about themselves
Yes, there are times when only death makes sense
And only pain makes me feel like I am alive.
I feel numbed
Numbed to the world
All I want is to feel again.

I know this:
There is a hope
Elusive as may be
And difficult to see or understand.
God, through Jesus,
Has made himself available
And even when it feels like he isn't there
Or doesn't care
He is. He does.
He hears me
And remembers EVERY thing I ever say to him.
I won't give up.

(WAILING WALL, WWW.24-7PRAYER.COM)
[LAMENT, THANKS]

Time to Mend

Tears at night
Pain at dawn
How is it that I can feel so alone?
Leaning on a staff
that's about to snap;
I bend.
I bow.
I break.
You create a barrier,
so my broken body, heart and soul
have time to mend.

(WAILING WALL, WWW.24-7PRAYER.COM)
[REPENTANCE]

The Meek

Blessed are the meek, for they will inherit the earth.

MATTHEW 5:5

I am sitting outside a kebab shop in San Antonio's West End at 4 A.M. I'm tired and hot. Four in the morning seems like a weird time to have chips and a Coke, but I need a break.

As I sit and eat, two workers from one of the bars come and sit next to me. Their job is to walk around all night selling their goods to drunk English holidaymakers. I guess this can be wearying—they look tired and a little emotional.

As the 24-7 team hangs around the West End offering to pray for people, we often get prayer requests that border on shallow and selfish: more money, a better sex life, winning the lottery, cheap tickets to a particular club. This pair tonight doesn't want any of that. They're not focused on themselves—their brokenness is for their granddad who has a terminal disease and will soon die.

They don't want me to pray for his healing—they have accepted the inevitable—but for him to have a good quality of life before he dies. I pray with them for their granddad, and then we hug and say goodbye. I am struck by their meekness, their humility—they want nothing for themselves. I pray that I will see them again.

The following is a collection of meek prayers—the prayers prayed by people who remember the world does not revolve around them. Prayers of praise, humbleness and brokenness.

To Have a Bath Is Freedom

Written by a young man who was recently released from prison after committing a number of violent crimes:

To have a bath
    is freedom,
to choose what you eat for breakfast
    is freedom,
to open a door when you want to,
    to walk to the shops,
to work, to rest, to watch television,
    to hug, to play, to travel, to pray.

God gives me freedom

He gives me freedom
    in my mind,
He helps me appreciate gentle things
    (to see beauty and goodness)
Most importantly, he helps me to love
Freedom is found in love

(UNITED KINGDOM)
[CELEBRATION]

You Are Simple

Despite my complexity, you are simplicity
Despite my pride, you are humility
Despite my frantic schedule, you show me how to be
Despite my hectic life, my crowded mind,
you are my peace

(WAILING WALL, WWW.24-7PRAYER.COM)
[THANKS]

No Wasted Prayer

No prayers it seems are wasted,
Every crumb is collected.
Every word spoken has some kind of life in it.
God uses everything.

(UNITED KINGDOM)
[THANKS]

Adultery

Father, I don't want to live in adultery anymore,
please show me the way to get out of this.

(UNITED STATES)
[REPENTANCE]

Confidence

دنا دثق من ده دلله يعد بالنسبة لي افضل توظيف. درجاء مساعدتي
للصلاد.

I am confident that God is preparing for me
the best employment possible.
Please help me to pray.

(EGYPT)
[REQUEST]

Just Be

Just be
With me
Don't struggle or push or try
Just be
With me

Be my child
Heir to my Kingdom
All that is mine
Is yours

Remember the tree?
I did it for you
So you could be
Be with me

The past has gone
It did, it was—it finished
The future
Can be, shall be, will be
You
and
Me

Just be
Be with me
Don't struggle or push or try
Just be
With me

(UNITED KINGDOM)
[MEDITATION]

saliga är de som är fattiga i anden, dem tillhör himmelriket

Jag prisar dig, Fader,
du himlens och jordens Herre,
för att du har dolt detta
för de visa och kloka och
uppenbarat det för de små.
Ja, Fader, detta var din goda
vilja. Allt har min Fader
överlämnat
åt mig,
och ingen känner
Sonen utom Fadern.
Inte heller känner
någon Fadern utom
Sonen och den som
Sonen vill uppenbara
honom för.
Kom till mig alla ni
som arbetar och bär på
tunga bördor så skall jag
ge er vila. Ta på er
mitt ok och lär av mig,
ty jag är mild och ödmjuk
i hjärtat, då skall ni
finna ro för era själar
ty mitt ok är milt och
min börda är lätt

saliga är de som sörjer, de skall bli tröstade saliga är de ödmjuka, de skall

arva jorden, saliga är de barmhärtiga, de skall få barmhärtighet...

Something I'm Not

Thank you for saving me from death at my own hands,
from self-mutilation and starving myself to be
something I'm not.
Thank you for saving me from depression
I never thought I'd be able to overcome.

(CANADA)
[THANKS]

Lost Momentum

I've made huge leaps in the last year and now
I feel at a standstill.
What should I do? Where should I go? Where next?
Please help. I'm a bit lost.

(UNITED KINGDOM)
[REQUEST]

Pray

Dear God, I want to pray.

(UNITED STATES)
[MEDITATION, REQUEST]

The Weight of All I Am Not

I'm so tired of failing.
So tired of despair.
I feel the weight of all that I am not.
I want to be grateful to God,
I want to be free from what holds me back.
I want to run a race of courage.
But my strength wanes.

(WAILING WALL, WWW.24-7PRAYER.COM)
[MEDITATION]

Walking Behind

Walking behind is OK
I watch your feet
If you turn
Will I run
Away?

(WAILING WALL, WWW.24-7PRAYER.COM)
[MEDITATION]

Use Me (If You Can)

Use me, Lord,
I'm here.
Use me if you can
There's nothing left
I'm empty
Alone
Nowhere to turn
And life is like
Chasing the wind
Use me, Lord

(CANADA)
[REQUEST]

From Silence

From silence I bring forth
what I cannot from sound.
Pen and paper fade away
but forever the song is written in my heart.

(SOUTH AFRICA)
[MEDITATION]

Who I Was Made to Be

I'm so good at being
everything but myself.

But this is not who I was made to be,
You don't look at me and see a bad job,
A mistake.
If all you made is beautiful,
Could I be too?

And in your tenderness
I hear you whisper my name.

(UNITED KINGDOM)
[MEDITATION]

Those Who Seek Righteousness

Blessed are those who hunger and thirst for
righteousness, for they will be filled.

MATTHEW 5:6

We are standing in the middle of the West End in San Antonio with workers whose job it is to entice people into their bars to drink as much as they possibly can. Hundreds of people stream by every minute. There is noise from the bars, drug dealers trying to sell their wares, drunks chanting and shouting. The smell of smoke and beer hangs heavily in the hot, humid air.

It's hard for these guys. Many of them work on commission and only get paid when they get people into the bar. Personality is everything, and all of them are chatty, enthusiastic and good at their jobs. We stand in their midst, talking and praying with them. After a long chat with a guy named Dave, we ask him if there is anything we can pray about for him. Very quietly and sincerely he says, "That I will find the truth."

In only a few words, Dave has summed up the heart-cry of a generation. He is hungry and thirsty for truth, truth that can only be found in the righteousness of Jesus Christ.

In the madness of life, what are we hungry and thirsty for?

Marriage

Oro por mi matrimonio.
Para que el amor conyugal, la comprension, el perdon y la felicidad
sean desde hoy una realidad en mi relacion
con mi esposa e hijos.

I pray for my marriage.
May love, understanding, forgiveness and happiness
be a reality from this day forward in my relationship
with my husband and my children.

(MEXICO)
[REQUEST]

Give Us Your Light

Danos tu luzentre tanta gente,
cada dia enseñame a ver tu rostro y tu luz.
Quiero estar en tu luz ser un destello de tu inmensidad

Give us your light,
teach us to see your face each day.
I want to be in the light, to be a reflection
of your immensity.

(SPAIN)
[MEDITATION]

Understand the Meaning

Padre te pido por Roberto llena su corazon con tu amor.
Que sienta Tu Presencia. Que comprenda lo que es relacionarse
con uno Dios maravilloso y no sentir mas aquel vacio en el pecho.
Trae salvacion a su alma, abra sus ojos espirituales y permita
que deje la religiosidad por tu genuina compania.
Padre, bendicele en todo y cuidalo del mal.
Te pido en el nombre de Jesus. Salvation to Roberto.

Father, I pray for Roberto—fill his heart with your love.
May he know your presence. May he understand the meaning
of a relationship with God and not feel emptiness in his heart.
Bring salvation to his soul, open his spiritual eyes,
may he exchange a life of religion for genuine
relationship with you.
Bless him and keep him from evil.
I ask this in the name of Jesus. Salvation for Roberto.

(SPAIN)
[INTERCESSION]

Living Water

I have no strength. I need living water.

(SPAIN)
[REQUEST]

A Tiny Army

A tiny army steps forth
Looking out on a huge dark night.
Says, "We're good to go, Sir."
A tiny army lifts its candles against the night
raises the lilting song of
A tiny army

And heaven opens
Where they walk
He breaks the night

(PORTUGAL)
[MEDITATION]

Cry for God

Set in us a cry for you
so deep inside we cannot find
the words we need.

(UNITED KINGDOM)
[LAMENT]

Five Senses of a City

Father, I pray that you'd reawaken the senses of my city

Eyes
Dull to the beauty of your creation
Would you restore sight?

Ears
Deafened by verbal abuse
Would you restore hearing?

Noses
Seared by the stench of sin
Would you restore our sense of smell?

Taste buds
Desensitized by blasphemy, alcohol and drugs
Would you make us hunger for pure flavors?

Bodies
Deadened by pleasure seeking, no longer able to feel true
joy Would you restore all five dimensions of our sensitivity
to you?

(UNITED KINGDOM)
[INTERCESSION]

Open My Mouth

Abre mi boca! Padre, abre mi boca para poder llegar
a mis compañeros de clase, para que te puedan conocer.
Ayúdame a superar mis miedos y mis complejos para que ya
no puedan ser de estorbo para tu obra.
Lléname de tu espíritu para predicar con denuedo.

Open my mouth! Father, open my mouth so that I may reach
my classmates, that they may know you.
Help me to overcome my fears, may my personal shortcomings
never interfere with your kingdom work.
Fill me with your spirit to preach with renewed zeal.

(SPAIN)
[REQUEST]

Sexual Temptation

I once had no problems with lust,
but now at almost every temptation, I fall.
Please help me to have the strength to resist!

(SWITZERLAND)
[REPENTANCE]

Release Me from Niceness

I like the comfort zone
I like to be popular
I settle with the few
I prefer to make small waves
I don't like being out of my depth
God, get me out of this
Release me from this niceness
Put me in the center of things
Where people will react to me
Because I tell them the truth
I'm scared. I don't want to look back when I am old
To see a life of lost opportunities
In which I haven't shaken the world
In a big or even a small way
God, help me to tell the truth
With love to all who will listen

(UNITED KINGDOM)
[REQUEST]

I Want to See You

Isn't it so easy to enjoy life and forget about God?
Then it is so easy not to enjoy life and be miserable . . .
It is hard to find a balance.
I feel so far from You, Lord and I am finding it hard to pray.
But no matter how I may feel,
I long for the day when I'll see You face to face.

(WAILING WALL, WWW.24-7PRAYER.COM)
[MEDITATION]

Doubting Evangelist

Lord, give me strength.
I feel like I'm all alone in my Christian growth.
I can't try to encourage my friends to follow you when I'm not too
sure myself.
Show yourself to me like you used to, please!
I feel like you're there but you are a fuzzy image to me.
Make yourself clear so that I am confident in you
and have confidence to prove your love to others.

(UNITED KINGDOM)
[REQUEST]

Jesus

I can't stop thinking about you, Jesus.
I can't get enough of you.
Will my craving ever be satisfied?

(UNITED KINGDOM)
[MEDITATION]

Viking Heart

Send not your foolish and feeble;
Send me your strong and your sane.
And I will wait for the man who will win me,
and I will not be won in a day.
I will not be won by weaklings
Subtle and suave and mild;
But by a man with the heart of a Viking
And the simple faith of a child.
Desperate, strong, and restless
Unthrottled by fear or defeat
To him will I give my treasure.

(NORWAY)
[MEDITATION]

Forsaken

The clock's ticking,
precious seconds of my life
Away.
Can you hear me when I pray?
Why aren't things going my way?
I'm screaming Your Name,
Needing answers and solutions,
Yet none come.
I'm waiting, waiting for
my turn,
And I'm losing the will to even want to try to pray . . .
Please don't leave me here
All alone . . .

(WAILING WALL, WWW.24-7PRAYER.COM)
[LAMENT]

For Divine Inspiration

God, I'm searching for something real. I need some inspiration here.
I've been groping around in the dark. Looking for some kind of spark.
You have provided again and again.
But this link between heart and words is lacking.
Help me get to the core of my emotions.
Help me get to the depths of my whole being.
There is nothing I want more than to be used, nothing else but you.
It is consummation, dissatisfaction with everything but you.
My life has cost too much to just throw it away.
Jesus, do something new. Get some art back into my world.

(UNITED STATES)
[REQUEST]

Searching

I feel as if I am searching in a huge city for one person.
Impossible?
I know I will eventually find you,
or maybe that's the wrong way around.
Perhaps I am running from you to keep myself hidden?

(CANADA)
[MEDITATION]

For Laughter

I don't wanna compromise anymore,
I don't wanna be lukewarm,
always striving, always trying to justify
always living under the expectation
the "you're not good enough"
the "why can't you be more like _____
or do more of _____"

I wanna come to you and receive freedom
to know what it is to be your child
you gave me laughter as a gift
so many times it's become lost and crushed

Revive, refresh, reform my soul
no longer living under the limits, the ceilings

BUT FREE TO LIVE
FREE TO BE ME

as you intended

(WAILING WALL, WWW.24-7PRAYER.COM)
[REQUEST]

Release from Porn

Jesus, I want to thank you for helping me to
break free from my porn addiction.
To get on with my life and seek a future with my wife,
with you at the center of every decision we will make.
I am free and no longer suffering.
Lord, I thank you and will praise you forever. Amen

(UNITED STATES)
[THANKS]

Make Me Clean

I hate who I am.
I am a living wreck without you.
Can you make me clean?

(CANADA)
[REPENTANCE]

If Only I Could

If only I could see
I would see eyes ablaze in eternity
see the Cross stretched over time
see the Son in glorious splendor

If only I could hear
I would hear rushing waters and gentle whispers
hear Love's command ring
hear You sing

If only I could feel
I would touch the angels that surround me
feel my Father's embrace
feel the blood cleansing white

If only I could know and understand
I would leave the world's way
cling to You above all else
know and understand wisdom and revelation

If only I could.

So I turn
to see
to hear
to feel
to know
and understand
Yahweh.

(SOUTH AFRICA)
[MEDITATION]

Turn Our Tables

Turn our tables; clean out the temple
The evidence of our materialism
The gathered sum of our achievements
Our precious shows of success

Take our superficiality,
Scatter our coins
Overturn our tables
Have we made you a commodity?

Are we prepared?
To lose everything.
To do your will.
Or is the price too high?

(WAILING WALL, WWW.24-7PRAYER.COM)
[REPENTANCE, REQUEST]

Compassionate, caring, loving God,
I am so sorry for the times I have
judged those who don't know you, then
I have been too proud or too scared to
talk to them. God please help me to
follow your example, to have more compassion
on them, to remember that they are not evil,
but just simply lost. Help me to be an
example of you, to show them that you
to you. God help me to be willing to go
out there and share your good news, not just
to my own prayer, to be willing to gee
give me a passion and a heart to be lost to be
faithful to them in prayer, to stand in the gap,
stay there in the cozy safe boiler room. God please
to intercede, to weep and groan for our Father.
God I know you are not dependant on
me. But you can carry give your plans without
me. But God I pray that I would be in a place
where I am helpful and useful to you. God
open my eyes to see opportunities you give me,
and give me courage, boldness and love to make
the most of those opportunities. Oh God, give me your
heart to be lost.

Amen.

Jesus

my LORD
my LOVER
my FRIEND

TRUTH · HOPE ·
STRENGTH · JOY
PEACE · CONFIDENCE

I HAVE ALL
IN YOU.

GRACIAS
THANK YOU
Thank you
Thank You!

LOVE.

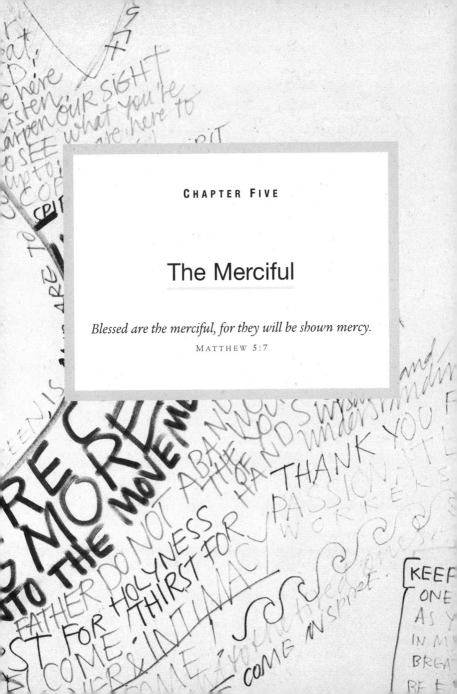

CHAPTER FIVE

The Merciful

Blessed are the merciful, for they will be shown mercy.

MATTHEW 5:7

Where I live, a prayer for mercy is often the same as an act of mercy.

We find Matthew passed out and lying in a pool of vomit outside a hotel entrance. Numerous policemen walk by and tell us to leave him there, but Matthew is obviously in need of serious help.

Matthew had too much to drink and is alone without ID. He continues to throw up and is shivering, pale and cold. There aren't enough dry clothes around, so several of us use our body heat to keep him warm. We clean up the mess around the hotel.

Unfortunately, it's not a simple matter to get Matthew to a hospital. A few more policemen pass by and look like they will continue to ignore him until they see the five of us taking care of him, unwilling to leave him there. They have a change of attitude and call an ambulance, which comes after a long time.

We talk to Matthew while we're waiting. Although he is quite sick, he is very grateful to us and says that we shouldn't have to be there with him—an attitude that seems to be shared by the policemen and the ambulance drivers. A couple of them laugh because they have never seen anything like us before.

We were able to *be* Jesus' love, answering a prayer for mercy with an act of mercy.

Telling Others

God, I pray that you will help me to go out and
tell someone about you.
And help me to live for you forever.
In Jesus' name, Amen.

(SIERRA LEONE, WEST AFRICA)
[REQUEST]

Living Water

This place, God, this town, that was once famous
for its life-giving waters—
let them flow once more.
Through the streets, the bins, the gutters, the drains,
on the beach,
in people's houses, the shops.
Let them flow once more.
We stand for life in this place, activity not apathy,
prayer not curse, celebration not mourning.
(Zephaniah 3:16-17)

(PORTUGAL)
[INTERCESSION]

For Hlupi

Hlupi was a three-year-old African girl with full-blown AIDS. She lived with her mother and grandmother in a tiny hut. Her mother also had AIDS and was so sick that she couldn't do anything for herself—Hlupi's grandmother had to bathe, dress, feed and care for her. The grandmother didn't have the strength to care for both her daughter and grandchild, so Hlupi was neglected. When Wendy, who wrote this prayer, visited the family, Hlupi watched her from the shadows of the doorway, too ashamed of the sores that covered her body to come out into the daylight.

Your timid and scared eyes,
Jewels in the wasteland of flaking ash.
The remains of Africa's selfish sins,
As you hide in the smoky darkness
Of your humble refuge

I wish with all of my broken heart
That you and I could exchange places.
Just that you might know what it's like
to be loved
to be healthy
to smile uninhibited
How I long to take you in my arms
And shelter your frail frame from loneliness and pain.
To wash your small child body with tears of love.
How much longer before Jesus takes you home?
Can you survive the battering of the storm?
How hard your innocence struggles to understand.
I pray for peace to envelop your soul.

(SOUTH AFRICA)
[INTERCESSION, LAMENT]

The Swoosh of an Angel Wing

Sometimes this place is like hell
Buy a shooter over the bar
13-year-olds in a hot-wired car
Arson and blades
Addiction and raids
Girls underage
Needles and AIDS
Suicide and sadness
Fear hate and loneliness
Jungle and garage
Abortions 'n miscarriage
Gold jewelry 'n the feds
Hooded tops and mopeds
Truancy and technics
MCs and vodka kicks
ADHD
Cold turkey
So here I stand
With bag in hand

Chips in pita bread
With a pickled egg
My bus is pulling up
I gotta Cherry Coke to sup
I've been emptying the ocean with a tea cup
How many times do I say
That at the end of a day like today
I've got nothing left to give except pray
Pray for this estate
A community of enemies and mates
Now another day's over for this fighter
I'm humming the tune to "Lighter"
Mooching under the scaffolding
Sensing the swoosh of an angel wing

(UNITED KINGDOM)
[MEDITATION]

Addiction

Dear Lord, thanks for the great day.
I pray for addicts who are still suffering,
for those who desire to stay clean
grant us the strength to stay clean and sober,
help to block every temptation that may
ruin our efforts for a new life.
Thanks for the cross, Jesus,
Thanks for listening to my prayer.

(SCOTLAND)
[INTERCESSION, REQUEST]

Mary Ate My Pizza

Hey, God. Tonight's going pretty well, thank you.
I pray that you'll give me the strength to
forgive Mary for eating my pizza.
I want to thank you for Mary—she's been the
No. 1 support through my Christian growth.
Thank you for sending her as an angel to me.
I pray that you'll super-glue me to your path
and not let me be influenced
by my non-believing friends.
But let me influence them like Mary has influenced me.
Help me to be a Mary.

(UNITED KINGDOM)
[REQUEST, THANKS]

Luck

*Dear God, I'm asking for a little bit of health for
my entire family,
and if possible a little bit of luck as well.
We have had so little of both in our lifetime.*

(UNITED STATES)
[INTERCESSION]

Healing

*Please pray for Kia.
She is two years old and has been diagnosed
with bone marrow leukemia.*

[REQUEST]

The following was scrawled over the original prayer:

The cancer's gone into remission and the doctors are gobsmacked!

(UNITED KINGDOM)
[PRAISE]

God's Brew

This prayer was taken from the unlikely prayer room at the
Buckner Ragsdale Brewery in Missouri. It meditates on a surprising
Bible verse: "Give beer to those who are perishing, wine to those
who are in anguish; let them drink and forget their poverty and
remember their misery no more" (Proverbs 31:6).

Buckner Ragsdale
This is an unusual place
Beer and Jesus
Who would have thought?

Lord,
I want to be a brewery
Where the right stuff is put in
Mixed with Your Spirit
And those who drink from it
Are changed

You have mixed us well here
You challenge our thinking
Christian or not
Mixing the "secular"
And the "sacred"
Where is the line?

The brew
Is You

It is potent
And easy to swallow

You said that beer is for those
Who are perishing
And wine for those
Who are in anguish
Let them drink and
Forget their poverty
And remember their misery
No more

Lord, mix us into a brew
That eases their misery
Use us
To warm their hearts
And change their perspective

(UNITED STATES)
[MEDITATION, REQUEST]

I Am a Beggar

I am a beggar
I stretch out my leprous hands
Marred, scarred, shaking, empty—
Will You hold them?

I am a beggar
My eyes are dim,
ever streaking my eyes
with bittersweet water
bewildered blue, ashamed—
Will You lift my head?

I am a beggar
Weak in body
Wounded in soul
Hungry in spirit—
Will You nourish me?

I am a beggar
My garments are torn
Patched too often
Stained with blood—
Will You look at me?

I am a beggar
Unseen and hiding
From my own guilt
Alone and empty—
Will You draw me out?

I am a beggar
In desperate pain
Unable to speak
The language of grace—
Will You heal me?

I am a beggar
With a bitter heart
Crawling to Your feet
Worshipfully
Grasping Your robe—
Will You touch me?

(SOUTH AFRICA)
[MEDITATION, REQUEST]

For the Poor

Jesus,
You modeled being the outsider who brings in the excluded.
We pray now for those who are forgotten,
ignored and excluded in prayer.
We pray for those who don't have people praying for them.
We pray for those who lack the very basics of life.
We pray for those who we do not know,
but who you know intimately,
whose ways we do not know, yet who encounter you.
Help us comprehend the infinity of a God,
who can comprehend and do what we're asking.

(WAILING WALL, WWW.24-7PRAYER.COM)
[INTERCESSION]

No Healing

Why did my mum die of cancer?
We thought she would be healed but it didn't happen
I am going to have to trust you, God
Help us
As a family we need you
Please walk with us in our pain and loss
I don't understand
I'm angry
I'll try not to blame you
I still love you

(UNITED KINGDOM)
[LAMENT]

God Sees the Hurt

I see the anger in your heart,
That pulls you down and tears apart,
The sense of peace within your soul,
Security that made you whole.

I know the pain that they don't see,
I see you struggling to be
what they expect, while deep inside
I count the tears you try to hide.

I hear each question in your mind,
Confusion as you daily find,
The certainties, forever near,
turn their back and disappear.

I'm here through these uncertain days,
and as you walk these unknown ways,
Believe tomorrow's just begun,
and trust the light that leads you on.

(WAILING WALL, WWW.24-7PRAYER.COM)
[INTERCESSION]

The Pure in Heart

Blessed are the pure in heart, for they shall see God.
MATTHEW 5:8

It's the beginning of another night for my wife, Tracy, and her friend Rachel in the West End. They walk for a while, having agreed with each other that if either of them saw somebody whom they particularly felt they needed to stop and talk to, they would tell the other.

Within a few minutes, they spot a group of girls, mostly dressed in red, some wearing devil's horns—a typical British hen party. They turn to each other at the same moment, smile and both say, "Shall we?"

Several of the girls are keen to chat, so they sit down at their table. One girl talks about her grandparents who have died. As she speaks, she begins to cry and is surprised by her own tears; this isn't something she usually cries about. The girl explains that she is normally very good at holding it all together.

A friend suddenly notices her tears and is confused. She becomes protective and jumps to her friend's defense, demanding to know what has been said that upset her. Rachel is quiet for a moment, having said nothing until now, and then gently responds, "It's not us that's making you cry."

"I know that," comes the reply. "It's God in you that's touching me."

Something about the purity of Rachel's heart had touched this girl. It was God in her; His beauty shining through.

Beautiful

We
can never pay back and

You
have never demanded

You
are beautiful!

Thanks

(SWEDEN)
[PRAISE]

Precious Things

Precious things are worthless
Precious things entrap the soul
Matter fills our bones

(PORTUGAL)
[MEDITATION]

For Guidance

God, first of all, I love you even if I don't show it,
Thank You that You love me and You do show it!
Continue to place things in my life to keep away the boredom.
You have given me abundance.
God, help me in my confusion and doubt.
Be my path, guide and light.

(NICARAGUA, CENTRAL AMERICA)
[REQUEST, THANKS]

My Generation

Gracias papa. Gracias por este cambio radical en mi vida.
No se como agradcertelo. Porfavor entrenanos a
esta neuva generacion
para demostrar a todo que existes. Señor.se que no
saben lo que se pierden.
Estamos dispuesto a parar al enemigo
y demostrar que estas vivo. Ayudanos. Amen.

Thank you, Father. Thanks for this radical change in my life.
I don't know how to thank you enough. Please train my generation
to demonstrate your existence. Lord, many do not know
what they're missing.
We are willing to stop the enemy
and demonstrate that you live. Help us.

(SPAIN)
[INTERCESSION]

A Hug

A hug drains away the weariness of the day.
A hug can hold both laughter and tears.
A hug brings you close to someone who cares.
A hug is a moment of peace.
A hug lets the soul fly into the realm of beauty.
A hug grants strength in support.
A hug brings hearts to touch.

(UNITED STATES)
[MEDITATION]

You in the Now

Though my situation changes,
and my knees are trembling
there is you . . . Always you

The questions I ask
the decisions I fail to make
the choices I am scared of
Does it matter? As long as there is you

(WAILING WALL, WWW.24-7PRAYER.COM)
[MEDITATION, PRAISE]

Gratitude for a Father's Love

Thank you
For being a father when I needed a father's touch.
For being a friend when I needed a friend's encouragement.
For being a comforter when I needed to know you were close.
For laughing with me when that is what I needed
And for crying with me when I felt most broken.
For loving me no matter what I've done and will do.
For scolding me as a gentle father scolds his child.
For your forgiveness, which I will always need.
For your amazing power when I needed to see your strength.
But most of all, my Father, friend, healer—
Thank you for paying the highest ransom for me.
For this I will always love you and seek you
with all of my heart and soul and strength and mind.

(UNITED KINGDOM)
[THANKS]

My Heart

Lord Jesus, please set my heart at peace again.
My emotions are confusing me.
I want to love you more and not be so easily swayed.

(AUSTRALIA)
[REQUEST]

HOLD ME LORD

You Are

Lord,
You are my soul's food and water
You are the courage that helps me face today
You are the hope that drives me on
You are the faith that keeps me trying
You are the strength that upholds me
You are the mercy that covers me when I err
You are the grace that sees past my faults
You are the joy that I reach out for
You are the source of patience in times of trial
You are the time that I always need
You are the honor that I work so hard for
You are the fulfillment of my heart's calling
You are the smile in my spirit when I wake up everyday
You are the hand that keeps me steady
You are the voice I always need to hear
You are the peace I am always searching for
You are the light that shatters darkness in my mind
You are the door I looked so hard to find
You are the inspiration for my dreams
You are the shelter I take from the storms of life
You are the provider of all my needs
You are the one who always calls me to return
You are the planner of all my plans
You are the love that makes me breathe
You are the truth I base my future on
You are my Father.

(SOUTH AFRICA)
[PRAISE]

My Hero

Written by a boy, age 8:

When I grow up I want to have God's heart because he's my hero.

(UNITED KINGDOM)
[REQUEST]

Rainbows

Written by a girl, age 6:

Thank you, God, for rainbows
Love, Holly

(UNITED KINGDOM)
[THANKS]

Not Alone

At times I wondered where you were,
wondered if you'd deserted me.
But you didn't, you were always there,
even when I couldn't feel you.
I can see the evidence of you running after me,
pursuing me.
God, I'm not running anymore, thank you.

(UNITED KINGDOM)
[THANKS]

Father and Son

My dad's rich
He's my hero
I'm taught, I'm trained, I'm straightened out
I'm a son
I've got a big dad
I revere him, he's so strong
He wins all our wrestling matches
I don't mind because
I'm a son
He makes me laugh, he brings peace,
when he's around I feel chilled
I'm a son
My dad never pops out for the evening,
He's always there for me
I'm a son
He pushes me, encourages me,
helps me to stand on my own two feet
Thank you, father
I'm your son

(IRELAND)
[PRAISE]

No Love Like Yours

A mi amado, no hay amor como el tuyo que
pueda llenar todo mi ser.
No anhelo nada más y a nadie mas.
Si por un momento o por alguna circunstancia mi amor
por ti disminuyese,
auxiliame con tu mano y vuelveme a ti porque
tu eres el Dios de mi salvación,
mi amor eterno, mi verdadero amor.

To my darling, there is no love like your love,
it fills my entire being.
I long for nothing more and no one else but you.
If ever my love for you grows cold,
reach out your hand and draw me back to you,
for you are my God and my salvation,
my love eternal, my true love.

(MEXICO)
[MEDITATION, PRAISE]

In Unapproachable Light

In unapproachable light You dwell
You are clothed with the sun
The rays of the morning go before You
Eternal destiny comes after One God
In Your beauty hides the secret knowledge
Of Yahweh's unrelenting love desires
In the midst of Your perfected holiness
A devouring fire, all-consuming passion
Your love is never-ending
I am consumed
In this passionate desire
To dwell in unapproachable light
All the days of my life

(SOUTH AFRICA)
[MEDITATION, PRAISE]

Job Offer

*I've been praying a lot about my future
and have just been offered the most amazing job!
Thank you, Lord!*

(UNITED KINGDOM)
[THANKS]

We, You

we keep asking
you keep doing
we keep falling
you keep catching
we forget to thank you
you forget our failings
we keep dying
you keep living
we keep hating
you keep loving
we keep trying
you keep helping
we're self-obsessed
you're us-obsessed
we keep straying
you keep calling
we keep wondering

you keep pointing
we keep praising
you keep saving
we don't tell people
you keep leading
we keep asking
you keep listening
we keep learning
you keep teaching
we keep forgetting
you keep reminding
we think you are amazing
you think we are too!

(UNITED KINGDOM)
[PRAISE]

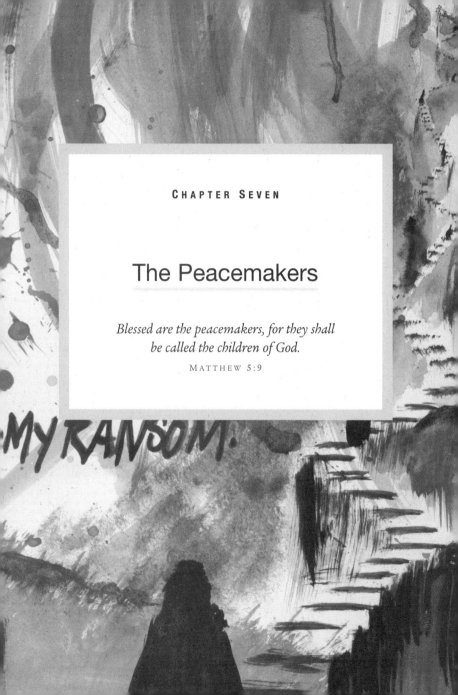

CHAPTER SEVEN

The Peacemakers

*Blessed are the peacemakers, for they shall
be called the children of God.*

MATTHEW 5:9

On another night, we are hanging around the West End and walk past Temptations Strip Club. One of the dancers is standing outside, and I decide to ask if there is anything we can pray about for her.

She is taken aback—usually men ask if she will dance for them, not if they can pray for her! In her shock and confusion, she reaches for the easy option: "Peace on earth." I say I will pray, and I take her prayer back to our prayer room to pin it up on the wall.

This beautiful young lady, just like you and me, knows that the world is not a peaceful place. And just like you and me, she believes it ought to be—that the world should be made right.

To pray for peace is also to ask the question, *How can I bring peace?* We are called to be peacemakers, to make daily decisions that bring peace to others. As we actively make peace, we grow closer to the Father's heart and demonstrate that we are, indeed, His children.

For a Nation

Father in heaven, hear the cries of your sons from Ghana.
We want economic stability and our currency to stop depreciating.
Help the many street children who have suffered abuse.
These children sell things they shouldn't have to.
Lord, turn back to us.
We need your guidelines and protection in all our endeavors.
Thank you, God, for hearing my prayers.

(GHANA, WEST AFRICA)
[INTERCESSION, REQUEST]

Anger

Lord, I repent for being angry and just so mad tonight.
I am sick of this and want it to stop.
I am sorry.

(WAILING WALL, WWW.24-7PRAYER.COM)
[REPENTANCE]

Baby Girl

Lord, thanks for blessing us with a little baby girl.
It's been hard at times becoming a parent,
but I thank you that we have the opportunity to bring her up
and I pray that she will grow up knowing that nothing
is impossible for you
and that you love her and everyone in the world.

(UNITED STATES)
[THANKS]

My Nation

Jesus, I cry out to you to come to my nation.
You are so beautifully sovereign,
you can change the heart of this land in a day if you wanted.
We need you, we desire and thirst for who you are.
Come, Jesus, we are super messed up.
Just need you to bring us to our knees
so that your healing and salvation will come to this land.

(NEW ZEALAND)
[INTERCESSION]

Free Me from This

I'm suddenly conscious of the battle within,
The war in which I'm taking the wrong side.
"Free me from this" (I cry to God)
and there's solitude in a crowded room.

(WAILING WALL, WWW.24-7PRAYER.COM)
[REPENTANCE]

God's Peace

Lord, I need you.
Help me to catch every chance I get
to talk about your love to this broken world.
Give me courage to bring your peace.
Peace beyond our questions.

(CANADA)
[REQUEST]

Your Name

I laid there in silence
listening to your name,
repeating over and over
doing my head in
hurting my brain

wishing that one day
you would be mine
together and in love
whispering your name

(UNITED KINGDOM)
[MEDITATION]

Your Voice

Your Voice is in the wind
Your Hand is in the storm
Your Love is in the rain
And Your Grace and never-ending Mercy
Always there to pull me through

(SOUTH AFRICA)
[MEDITATION]

Brick Wall

I often feel like I'm banging my head against a brick wall
with one of the girls I work with.
It's hard to see how her situation can ever change.
But this week we were able to talk really openly
about some of the things in her life
and it felt like a real breakthrough.
Thank you, God!

(UNITED KINGDOM)
[THANKS]

The Silence of God

Ahh . . . the Silence of God
So silent
So God

(WAILING WALL, WWW.24-7PRAYER.COM)
[MEDITATION]

Shine

The sweet one walked in
I knelt down and she kissed me
She is one of God's children
Elegant in poverty
Her mother was going to jump in front of a train
But found Jesus instead

Later another takes my hand
She falls asleep while praying for her nation
I have never seen such beauty
In all these faces
I cannot wait to get to heaven
To see them shining again

(ARGENTINA)
[MEDITATION, THANKS]

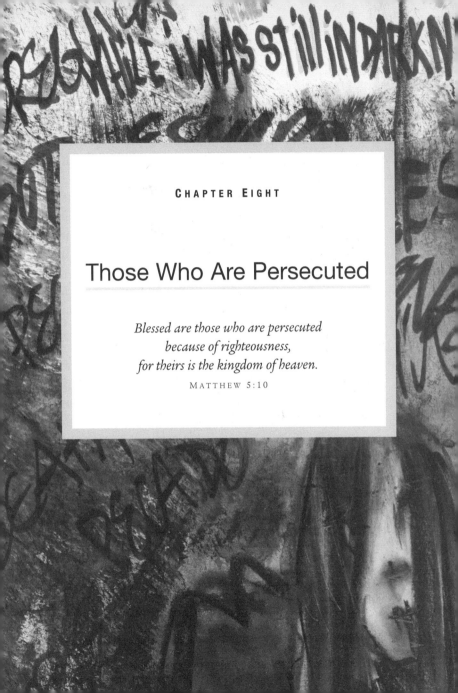

Those Who Are Persecuted

Blessed are those who are persecuted
because of righteousness,
for theirs is the kingdom of heaven.

MATTHEW 5:10

Finding a fitting story for this final chapter from our West End experiences eludes. The Scripture in Matthew 5:10 tells me that those who are persecuted because of righteousness are blessed, but thankfully we have not been subjected to persecution—other than some people thinking we are a little odd!

But in other parts of the world, there are people who suffer torture and even death because they will not save their own life on this earth if it means denying their faith in the One who has given them life. They try so hard to live right and honor God. They don't always understand the reason for their suffering or why people misunderstand them, but they endure, holding on to the promise that the kingdom of heaven belongs to them.

Sometimes I am fearful of walking the streets. There are nights when I don't want to go out and would rather just stay and pray in the comfort of our crazy little prayer room. But I keep going because I am absolutely convinced that God hears our prayers, and this spurs me on to carry Christ to the world we live in. And so, like those who live under the threat of persecution, I also hold on to the promise that the kingdom of heaven belongs to us.

Abandoned

Can you hear me when I pray?
Why aren't things going my way?
I'm screaming Your Name
Needing answers and solutions
Yet none come.
I'm waiting, waiting for
my turn
I crash and burn.
It's not fair!
You've abandoned me in my despair
My darkest hour,
Showing neither Your glory nor Your power
Do You not care?
Every bone in my body aches
Again and again I make the same mistakes . . .
Has grace run out for me
Our contract ended, down the pan
Though it's sealed in blood
The blood of the Son of Man?
Lessen the burden, Lord
I can't take it much longer
I'm growing weaker, not stronger!
I get farther and farther from You every day
And I'm losing the will to even want to try to pray . . .
Please don't leave me here
All alone . . .
Jesus, come back to me
Please stay!

(WAILING WALL, WWW.24-7PRAYER.COM)
[LAMENT]

Homeless

Why can people never see me for who I am?
Why do you have to bring me back to no-home situation?
Help me experience that my refuge is in you, please, God, help me.
I pray sanctuary for my family, my people.
Help me in my desperation.

(WAILING WALL, WWW.24-7PRAYER.COM)
[LAMENT]

Abuse

Jesus, I feel so far away from you.
Why is this happening to me?
You and I both know that I am telling the truth.
Why are you allowing this to happen?
Will I have to bury my children before someone does something?
Stop him from hurting them anymore PLEASE.

(UNITED STATES)
[LAMENT, REQUEST]

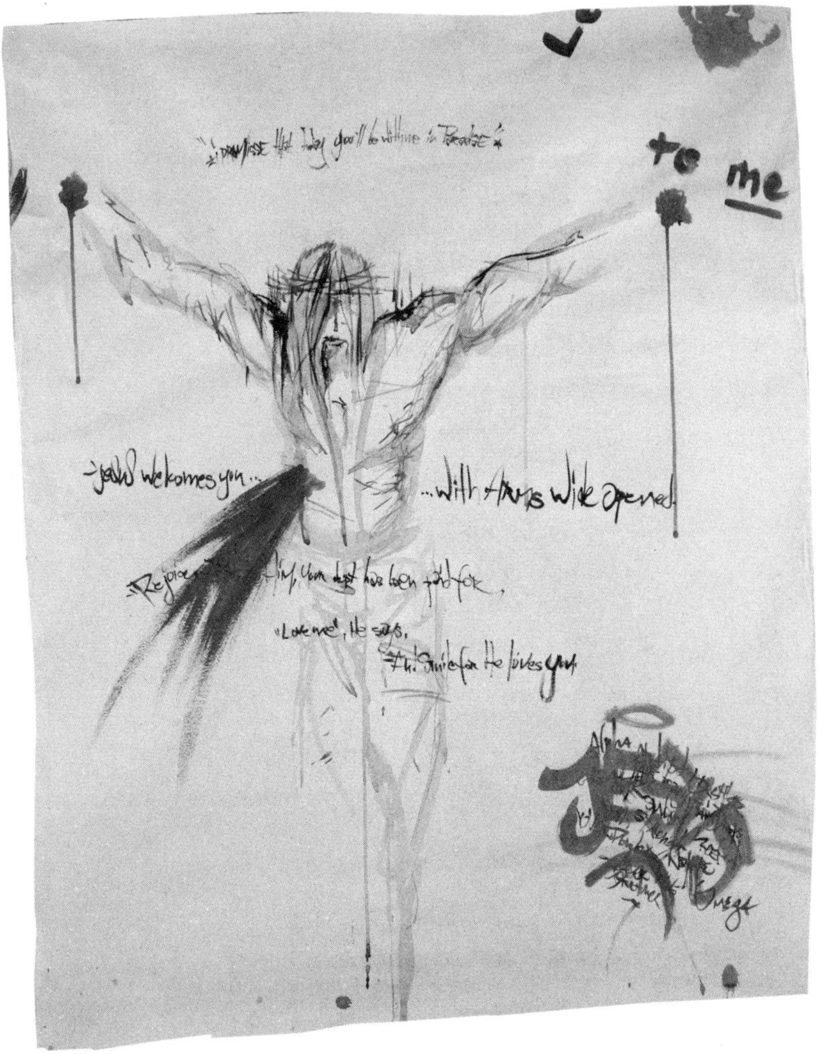
to me
Jesus welcomes you...
...with Arms wide opened.
"Love me", He says.

When You're Weary

I know your pain
And I am here.
I know you are tired
You have given up trying
Love seems impossible
Grace incomprehensible
And you have lost your peace.
I am here.
Come to Me
Sit in My presence
Show Me your fears
And tell Me your troubles
I will listen.

Give Me the pieces
And I will help you
Love again.
My child,
Be with Me,
and I will give you
true rest
for your soul.

(SOUTH AFRICA)
[MEDITATION]

New Generation

Que el enemigo no robe a esta nueva generacion
y que seamos una generacion fuerte y sin limites.
Que paremos al enemigo hacienda lo que haga falta
para demostrar que CRISTO VIVE!!!
Y no esta en una cruz clavado.
RESUCITO!

May the enemy stop robbing this new generation.
May we be a strong generation without limitations.
May we do whatever necessary to stop the enemy from advancing
to demonstrate the LIVING CHRIST!!!
He is no longer nailed to the cross.
HE HAS RISEN!

(SPAIN)
[INTERCESSION]

List of Prayers

Meditation

About the Compiler

Brian Heasley lives with his wife, Tracy, and two sons, Ellis and Daniel, on the European island of Ibiza. He is establishing a 24-7 Boiler Room in the town of San Antonio, which has more bars, pubs and clubs per square mile than anywhere else on the European continent. Previously, he led an innovative church in Norfolk, England, called DC3. Brian is a member of the 24-7 Prayer international leadership team and, over the years, has been involved in movements to pioneer Christian mission in emerging culture. He has a passion for clear, relevant communication and feels most alive when hanging out with people who are not yet Christians.

About 24-7 Prayer

24-7 Prayer started by accident in September 1999 when a bunch of young people in England got the crazy idea to pray nonstop for a month. God turned up, and they couldn't stop until Christmas! Since then, the prayer meeting has spread into other countries, denominations and age groups. Hundreds of nonstop prayer meetings now link up on the web to form a unique chain of prayer.

There are three dimensions to the movement: First, we're a network of prayer rooms determined to pray like it all depends on us and live like it all depends on God, until the tide turns in our generation. Second, a missions movement quickly arose out of the prayer rooms as we received requests to take teams to the "high places" in youth culture to serve. Third, we run Boiler Rooms—or houses of continual prayer (24-7-365)—which are like postmodern monasteries.

Participating prayer rooms pledge to pray 24 hours a day for a week or more in a dedicated prayer room. The prayer passes from location to location in a never-ending flow linked up by the 24-7 Prayer website—we are a virtual community praying in real locations. *Right now someone somewhere is praying 24-7.*

24-7 Prayer is steered internationally by a round table of equals who represent all the national bases and partner organizations. The term "round table" dates back to the legend of King Arthur. Some people think that he had the following phrase engraved on the round table at which his knights convened: "In serving one another we become free."

Engaging the Silence of Unanswered Prayer

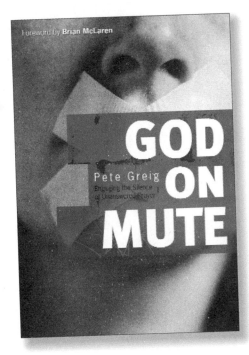

God on Mute
978.08307.43247

[24-7 TITLES]
WWW.24-7PRAYER.COM

Pete Greig, the acclaimed author of *Red Moon Rising*, has written his most intensely personal and honest book yet in *God on Mute*, a work born out of his wife Samie's fight for her life. Greig asks the timeless questions of what it means to suffer and to pray and to suffer through the silence because your prayers seem unanswered. This silence, Greig relates, is the hardest thing. The world collapses. Then all goes quiet. Words can't explain, don't fit, won't work. People avoid you and don't know what to say. So you turn to Him and you pray. You need Him more than ever before. But somehow…even God Himself seems on mute. In this heart-searching, honest and deeply profound book, Pete Greig looks at the hard side of prayer, how to respond when there seem to be no answers and how to cope with those who seek to interpret our experience for us. Here is a story of faith, hope and love beyond all understanding.

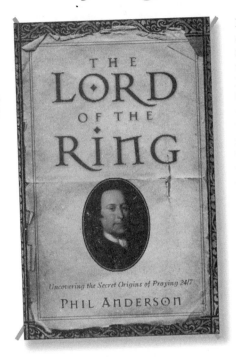